P₁

MW00491743

Ellis & Myra

From:

David & Pat

Date:

Dec 2003

Myra & Ellis...thanks for listening to life!

Listen to Life with Dr. Joey Faucette

The First Book

Connecting You With God's Love Through Everyday Stories

I dedicate this book to God whose unconditional love and persevering patience overwhelm me daily, and to my wife, Rowan, and daughters, Rebekah and Elizabeth, who have taught me how to truly listen to life today for what God has to say.

Acknowledgments

Most acknowledgements I've read start off something like, "There's no way I can acknowledge all the people who contributed to this book." Now I know what they mean. There really is no way!

What I mean is if I really stop and think about it, I've been writing this book most of my life which means hundreds, maybe thousands, of people deserve acknowledgement. Since I can't do that, let me name a few with apologies to those humble people I leave out.

First, this book belongs to God. I'm more a co-author with God than anything else. The ideas belong to God. The mistakes are mine. Listeners and readers regularly ask me, "How do you come up with all that material?" referring to our weekday syndicated radio show and newspaper column from which this book is drawn. Always I say, "It's God's material and my lifestyle of listening to my life for what God has to say." Thank you, God!

Second, this book belongs to my family. When it seemed like this idea was a dream hatched in a pipe and nobody believed in it, my wife, Rowan, always said, "With God's help, you can do it. I believe in you." Our two daughters, Rebekah and Elizabeth, have followed in her footsteps. My mother gave me the gift of writing and my father gave the encouragement to do what he never did—"Get an education, son. Nobody can ever take that away from you." Thank you, family!

Third, this book belongs to the First Baptist Church of Danville, Virginia. These people of God have encouraged and prayed for me as I have sought God's will with the various expressions of this ministry. Some of them saw the potential for this book the first time I shared the opportunity for the radio show with them. Because of the sensitive discernment and earnest desire of these my spiritual companions, this book is yours to read. Thank you, church!

Fourth, this book belongs to the Board of Directors of *Listen to Life* and all the listeners and readers, but especially Gene Saunders of McCain Printing in Danville, Virginia. Because of the vision of the men and women of our Board, you can read this book. Because of Gene Saunders' courage, this book is in print. And because you're reading and listening, I want you to know how humbled I am by your allowing God to speak through me to you. Thank you, friends!

Contents

Listen to Life with Dr. Joey Faucette

The First Book

*Connecting You With
God's Love Through
Everyday Stories*

Introduction

Are you listening to life?

As a two-year-old, our older daughter was determined to interrupt my precious moments of important newspaper reading.

"Daddy, I want to tell you something," she said.

"Go ahead," I replied never moving the paper.

"Daddy, I want to tell you something," she said, only this time with a little more urgency.

"Go ahead I said," still not moving the paper.

Smashing my paper with her tiny hands, she said, "Daddy, I want you to listen with your eyes."

There are so many things in life that seem important to us. So many things that we feel like we have to do at least two things at once—reading and listening—every waking moment.

But there are some things in life that need our undivided attention, our ears and our eyes. They demand that we listen. Our children are one. God is another. And I'm convinced that God speaks to us through our children and through life events that seem innocent enough on the surface but actually cradle

1

God's spiritual desire to connect us with a love that's beyond our craziest dreams and wildest imagination.

I know because I've been connected with God's love through my family and other life events that seemed trivial at the time, but on reflection spoke the whispering voice of God. Now I'm no more special or spiritual than you. I'm just someone who had the newspaper smashed by his daughter, listened to that life event, and decided God was in it.

I believe you can do the same. I believe that you can listen to your life, hear God whispering love to you, and connect with that love. And that's the purpose of this book—to connect you with God's love through everyday stories.

You can read this book alone or with a group of friends. By reading it alone, you can spend some time with each story, think about the reflection questions after each story, and even jot down your thoughts and feelings. Or, you can read this book and then get together once a week with a group of friends, talk about the story for that week, (there are enough for a year), and then discuss the reflection questions.

My hope for you is that by reading this book, you'll say to yourself, "Hey! That's happened to me before!" or "I never thought about it that way." Either way, I hope that you'll start listening to life today for what God has to say—with your ears and your eyes…and your spirit.

What's the most loving thing you can do today?

W hen my wife was pregnant with our first child, she really wanted a certain kind of baby crib. She took me to the "baby store" and pointed out every little detail she loved about it. She could see her little darling sleeping in that very crib.

Well frankly, I didn't have enough money to buy it, but I really wanted to buy it. So I decided to sell my shotgun that I had received from Santa when I was a teenager so that I could buy that baby crib. On my way to the pawn shop, I stopped by to visit a friend who said he wanted it so I sold the shotgun to him and bought the crib. My wife loved it!

About twelve years later, on my fortieth birthday, my wife threw a huge birthday party for me. After everyone left, she took me into my home office and said, "There's one more thing. Here's your birthday present" and she handed me my shotgun that I had sold to buy the baby crib. She got it back from my friend who had kept it all those years.

Without a doubt that was the most loving thing she could have possibly done for my fortieth birthday. That gun now hangs on my home office wall as a daily reminder of how much my wife loves me.

3

Listen to Your Life

1. What's the most loving thing your spouse, or someone else, has done for you?

2. What's the most loving thing God has done for you?

3. What's the most loving thing you can do for someone today?

What are you looking for in life?

I really enjoy feeding the birds in winter. I set up a bird feeder in our backyard every winter. My problem is that squirrels love bird feeders, too.

I waged war on the squirrels one winter. I borrowed an air rifle, and started looking for the mangy "tree rats." I looked for the squirrels every time I walked by our bay window, just waiting for them to show themselves so that I could grab the rifle, sneak outside around the corner of our home, and surprise and shoot them. I even put our daughters on alert—"Girls, let me know if you see a squirrel on our bird feeder."

That is, until our younger daughter said, "Daddy, we used to look out the window for pretty birds. Now we look for ugly squirrels."

When she said that, I realized that all the joy of my bird feeder was gone. That I wasn't looking for pretty birds and their magnificent colors any more, but ugly squirrels that I could shoot.

It's easy to see only the ugly squirrels in life, isn't it? To look for and shoot bushy-tailed thieves who steal our joy.

It's easy to stop looking for the beautiful in life, to cease listening for the lovely songs. To miss the brilliant colors of the world around us.

Today, put down your weapon, stop looking for the ugly, and look for the beautiful in life. It's there…if you're listening to life today for what God has to say.

Listen to Your Life

1. What "squirrely" problems are you looking at?

2. What beautiful solutions are you looking past?

3. What does God want you to see?

Are you listening for God?

Our younger daughter said to me during a televised football game, "This is like a baseball game."

"No, sweetheart," I replied, "this is far different from a baseball game." And I went on to lecture her on the differences in the two games—the shapes of the balls, the number of players, the way you score points. Having satisfied myself, then I asked her, "Do you understand better now?"

"Yeah," she said, "but what I mean is the music is like a baseball game."

At that very moment—underneath the players' smashing each other, the coaches' barking plays, and the announcers' analysis—there came the music; the same music she had heard while we watched an Atlanta Braves game together. The music, one of those songs played to rev up the crowd, had been there all along, but I hadn't heard it. I wasn't listening carefully enough to hear it. But she listened and made the musical connection between two very different yet similar sports.

It's easy for you and me to miss the music of life, isn't it? It's easy for us to not listen to God's melody playing through the many different scores of our lives.

It's far more convenient for us to hear people smashing

each other or barking orders at each other. We even listen to paralysis by analysis—people telling us what to think and what to listen to.

And still the music plays, it's measured sound and silence, rhythm and rest, wanting to connect with our spirits. All we need to do is listen to life today for what God has to say and experience the music.

Listen to Your Life

1. What's your favorite kind of music?

2. Why do you enjoy that kind of music?

3. How does God touch your spirit through this kind of music?

Are you a creature of habit?

A ny time I go out of town and stay overnight in a hotel, after checking in, the first thing I do is unpack. I set out my toothbrush and toothpaste on the left side of the sink with a cup for water. My hairbrush, hair spray, and anti-perspirant go on the right side of the sink, just like they are at home. It's my way of making my new environment more like home.

On one trip, the cleaning person came into my room, cleaned the sink area, and rearranged my things. When I returned I wandered, "Who's been in my room?"

Then I realized that it was the cleaning person who had been in my room and that she was just doing her job and accidentally moved my stuff. I had to laugh at myself because I was so stuck in my comfort zone that all I could see was that my stuff was moved. I completely ignored the great job she had done cleaning. So I looked around the room and noticed how clean the carpet was, how dust-free the tables were, and how sparkling the sink was.

Like me in my hotel room, we get so stuck in our spiritual comfort zones that we think God can only speak to us in certain, predictable ways of our own choosing. But when it's soul-cleaning time, sometimes our spiritual things get rearranged. We only notice that God moved our stuff, missing the great job of cleaning up our messes God did.

Step outside of your spiritual comfort zone and notice how sparkling clean God wants to make your spirit. Then listen to your life for some different ways God wants to speak with you.

Listen to Your Life

1. Reflect on your daily habits. Name one thing that you do the same just about every day.

2. Now reflect on your spiritual habits. Name one spiritual habit that you have.

3. If God wanted to say something about life differently to you, how could God speak so that you would listen?

When do you stop?

It was one of those days for me. (I'm sure you've had at least one before.) I woke up that morning feeling like I was running behind before I even got out of bed. The morning was a blur with phone calls, drop-in visits, email—you get the idea. Then there was a lunch meeting. Then there came an emergency call from the hospital. I was needed there immediately.

So I got in my car and noticed the orange warning light came on my gas gauge again. I had seen it a couple of times the day before, but not really paid it much attention. "I don't have time to stop for gas," I thought.

Then the craziness of that thought hit me. Either I could take a few minutes and stop for gas at a station now or lose a lot of time by getting stranded on the side of the road later.

I pulled into a gas station, and it's a good thing I did. My car coughed twice and quit. I slipped the transmission into neutral and coasted up to the pump, feeling very blessed to have stopped when I did.

The next time you don't have time to stop for spiritual fuel, remember—sooner or later you will stop. Either you can choose to take a minute now by praying or meditating or reading a good book. Or, you can crash and burn your spirit by mistaking yourself for a spiritual perpetual motion machine. If you do, you'll lose lots of minutes later when you are forced to stop.

Since you're going to have to stop and refuel your spirit anyway, make it sooner rather than later. So go ahead and stop now.

Listen to Your Life

1. When was the last time you chose to stop and refuel your spirit?

2. When was the last time you didn't choose to stop and refuel your spirit, but had to anyway?

3. Which experience was more spiritually satisfying for you? Why?

Do you ever feel like you're losing it?

O ur older daughter was teaching our younger daughter how to inline skate. They were out on our driveway, which has a pretty good slope to it. Our younger daughter finally let go of her big sister's hand and started skating on her own. But going down the slope she started going too fast and lost control. As she lost control, she stepped off the driveway and over into the grass.

Our older daughter watched all of this stopping and starting very carefully. Then she skated over to her little sister, put a hand on her elbow, and held it there until she got her balance and could keep it. Pretty soon our younger daughter was skating on her own—thanks to her big sister's help.

Do you ever feel like you're losing it as you skate through life? Do you try to take control, lose it, and stumble to get it back? Maybe it's time for you to stop and ask God to put a hand on you until you get your balance.

Like our older daughter watched her little sister, God's watching you very carefully and is ready to help. In fact, as you're reading this story, God's coming over to you in love, wanting to touch you and hold you until you get your life's balance and can keep it. Pretty soon you'll be skating on your own—thanks to God's help.

13

Listen to Your Life

1. When have you felt out of control lately?

2. How did you regain your life balance? Or, did you?

3. Did you ask God to help? Why? Why not?

Is a picture worth a thousand words?

I keep a tiny black-and-white picture in my office. It's one of those small pictures with the pinking shear cut around the edges that were in vogue a few years ago. (Okay, more than a few years ago.)

In the picture, I'm about a year old, dressed in what looks like an Easter outfit—white shirt and shoes, plaid jacket, bow tie, and one of the sharpest looking caps you've ever seen. I'm standing on my grandparents' couch in their pine-paneled den, flanked on one side by my mother and the other by my father. Each of them has an arm around me. My mother's arm is around me for a loving hug. My father's arm wraps around me to keep me from falling off the couch.

I keep this childhood picture in my office as a reminder of my life before now. It reminds me that I've not always been where I am now. God's grace has been with me through a lot of years, loving me at whatever age I find myself. It reminds me that I've had a lot of help along the way. God through my parents' protection has seen me through some potentially dangerous situations. And this picture reminds me that it's my turn now as a father to wrap my arms of affection and protection around our daughters. And that as I do so, they are connected with the loving, gracious protection of God.

A picture really is worth a thousand words, isn't it?

Listen to Your Life

1. What picture of yourself do you especially treasure?

2. What is it about that picture that you particularly enjoy?

3. Where is God in that picture?

When does God come alive for you?

It was one of those snows that you remember for a long time. It was a large enough snow to make a huge snowman. My wife, daughter, and I did just that—rolling and piling snow into this six-foot snowman. We gave him ginger snap eyes, a carrot nose, stick arms, and chocolate chip cookie buttons. My daughter insisted we put a hat on him. And, of course, we named him Frosty.

You see, I had read Frosty to our daughter while we watched the snow fall. So we had to name him Frosty.

After we finished our Frosty, we stood back and admired him. As we did, she asked, "Daddy, when is he gonna come alive?" She remembered the story.

"I don't know, honey. We'll have to watch and wait," I said.

How do you tell your daughter who believes in the magic of an old silk hat that it's not real? That the story is just a fairy tale written to entertain children?

The next day brought the same question: "Daddy, when is he gonna come alive?"

"I don't know, honey. We'll have to watch and wait," I said. I knew my answer would not satisfy her the next day, but what else could I say?

When the next day came, it brought the same question as before, "Daddy, when is he gonna come alive?"

All I could think of was a miserable, "I don't know, honey."

But she was ready with an answer even if I wasn't.

"I know when he's gonna come alive, Daddy," she said. "He comes alive when we're not looking."

If you're looking for God to come alive, watching and waiting in a cold and frozen world, keep looking and believing even when you're not so sure. Keep asking, "When is God gonna come alive?"

If you're looking for God to come alive, remember—God can come alive even when you're not looking.

Listen to Your Life

1. When have you felt that God wasn't alive in your frozen world?

2. What was your watching and waiting like?

3. What can you listen to God now saying to you through that life experience?

Do you ever forget what's really important?

My wife and I went away for a weekend to a mountain lodge. I was sitting in a lobby outside of a gift shop waiting for her. I picked up a newspaper, found the business section, and started scanning the stock reports. (I was overcome with that urge we men suffer when we go shopping—the urge to redeem wasted time with something we consider important.) The light was dim in the room so I really had to concentrate.

A teenaged girl was sitting on a sofa across from me. All of a sudden another teenaged girl fell down on the sofa and the two girls started giggling. I heard them but tried to ignore them and kept looking at my stock reports. Then their mother jumped on the sofa, lying down across the two girls. Well then, they started laughing so loudly that I couldn't concentrate on my stock reports. I looked up just in time to see another woman pile on the sofa and then they were laughing way too loud and I was annoyed, even getting angry…

…until I thought, "Boy, they're having fun!"

So I started smiling, put down my newspaper, and laughed with them.

It's really easy to assume that what we think is important is the most important part of life to others as well. Do you ever forget what's really important? I did. And I suspect you do, too.

So let's listen to life today for what God has to say and have some fun.

Listen to Your Life

1. Remember a time when someone near you was having fun and you were distracted. What did you think? How did you feel?

2. What was so important to you at the time?

3. What do you think God would have chosen in your situation—the fun or what was so important to you at that time?

Where are you planted?

Do you ever feel cut off from life? At work or in your family or with your friends, you can feel cut off from everyone, including God.

A friend of mine was traveling through Ireland with a tour group. They were driving by bus through the beautiful countryside, admiring the rolling hills and green pastures.

My friend noticed that trees bordered the road. The more she looked at them the more she realized that they were all planted and grown the exact distance apart. She asked her tour guide about the trees.

"Oh yes," the tour guide told her. "Those trees were originally fence posts cut from trees. They were planted exactly five feet apart as fence posts. But the soil is so rich here that the planted fence posts started sprouting limbs and eventually grew into trees again."

Remember these fence posts that grew into trees again the next time you feel cut off from life at work or in your family or with friends. God can give you some rich soil where you're planted, so rich that your spirit can grow again. Just listen to life today for what God has to say and you'll grow.

Listen to Your Life

1. Recall a recent time when you felt cut off from others whether at work or in your family or with your friends. What did you feel and think at the time?

2. How did God meet you in your feelings and thoughts and grow your spirit again?

3. What did you learn from that experience that will help you grow next time you feel cut off?

What kind of chocolate bunny
is your favorite?

When I was a child, my Grandmother Faucette gave me a chocolate bunny every spring. I always looked forward to getting it, but there were some chocolate bunnies I liked better than others.

Some years she gave me a hollow chocolate bunny. Now I really liked the chocolate, but when I bit into it, well, I was disappointed because there was nothing but air inside of it. I really appreciated the chocolate bunny, but...

Other years she gave me a marshmallow-filled chocolate bunny. I never could tell just by picking up the bunny if it had air or marshmallow because the marshmallow is as light as air. So when I bit into it, I was excited because the bunny had something inside. But marshmallow does get a little old after a few bites.

My favorite years were those when my grandmother gave me a solid chocolate bunny. My excitement began the moment I touched the bunny because I could always tell when I picked it up if it was solid chocolate. It was the heaviest. Those bunnies were the same on the inside as on the outside—chocolate all the way through.

Just as my grandmother chose which chocolate bunny to

buy, so you and I choose how to spend our lives. We can choose to appear to be filled with God's love, but when life takes a bite out of us, we're hollow. We can choose to appear to be filled with God's love, but when life chews on us, we lose flavor quickly. Or, we can choose to be solid all the way through so that as life nibbles on us, God has filled us thoroughly with all the sweet goodness of divine love.

Listen to Your Life
1. Who was someone special in your life that gave you regular gifts?

2. In remembering those gifts, which ones were your favorites? Why? Which ones did you like, but prefer the others more? Why?

3. What gifts does God give you? How can you choose to become solid in your spirit through these gifts?

Do you want to be a millionaire, or are you already one?

One Sunday night recently our family was watching TV and a promo came on for *Who Wants to be a Millionaire?* And I asked my wife and daughters, "Do any of you want to be a millionaire?"

Our younger daughter, lying in the floor doing something like reading a magazine or coloring, never looked up and said, "I'm already a millionaire."

"Oh really," I said. "How do you figure that?"

"Well, I have you and Mama and my sister," she said, "and Nana and Papa and the rest of my family. Then there's my teacher and all my friends at school and church. Then there's Charlie our dog, and Maybelle and Norman our cats, my fish, and my horse. And most important of all, I have God in my heart. All of these are my million.

"People are more important than money, Daddy. Anybody can get money. But God is the most important of all."

That was quite a huge statement from such a little girl! All I could think of to say was, "You're right, honey."

But then my mind started perking on alternative game shows like *Who's Already a Millionaire?* Contestants could compete for the chance to talk with Regis about how God has blessed them with families and friends, pets and perks of life. Then they could share about why God is most important of all.

So what do you think—is there a market for my show?

Probably not?

Okay, instead of a game show, let's you and I play *Who's Already a Millionaire?* in our daily lives. Let's live as if we're already millionaires, because, if you use our daughter's "gold standard," we are! Just listen to life today and count your assets.

Listen to Your Life

1. Do you want to be a millionaire, or are you already one?

2. Count your assets today—people, not dollars.

3. Decide how you will remember today that God is most important.

What's forever with you?

I'm sure you watched with a lot of interest like I did last year when two sisters played in the semifinals at Wimbledon. Sisters Serena and Venus Williams played one another. It was the first time in over 100 years that two sisters competed against one another at Wimbledon. Their father didn't even attend the match because, I mean, who would he pull for?

The media interviewed Serena and Venus before the historic match. What really stuck with me was Venus' response to playing her sister at Wimbledon—"Family is forever. Tennis is just a game."

These two sisters virtually grew up with tennis rackets in their hands. They excel at tennis because of an intense competitive drive and hours of practice. But their love for winning, and they have both won a lot, hasn't skewed what's really important to them. "Family is forever. Tennis is just a game."

Can you imagine how wonderful the world would be if more of us listened to our lives, used the same "forever" priority criteria as Venus, and lived accordingly? We would all be at peace in our relationships as individuals and nations. We would all have plenty to eat and appropriate housing. We would all have what God intended.

Listen to your life today for what God has to say and decide what's forever with you.

Listen to Your Life

1. Do you remember which of the Williams sisters won that historic match at Wimbledon?

2. What's forever with you? And what's just a game?

3. How do you live into your "forever?"

What's your noise level like?

I was sitting in my favorite recliner at home, trying to have a conversation with my wife. She was seated in the chair next to me with only a lamp table in between us.

Suddenly I realized that I was yelling to be heard. So I listened around the room for a moment and figured out why. First, the TV was on, blaring through our speaker system. Now it had to be on loud enough to be heard over the fan that was blowing hot air from the gas logs. Because the gas logs, which dry out the air, were on, we were running a humidifier with its fan blowing. Throw in a couple of daughters talking, and its no wonder I was yelling.

So I got up out of my recliner and turned off the humidifier, turned back the fan blowing hot air from the gas logs, turned down the TV, and said, "Shhh" to our daughters. Then I sat back down, smiled at my wife, and said, "There, that's better."

You know, the noise level in our spirits makes us yell some times—"Hey God! Where are you?" Noises like worries at work, concerns about a teenager or an aging parent, suspicions about your spouse or, unpaid bills and the list goes on.

Get up from where you are and start turning down the noise in your spirit today. Then you won't have to yell at

God…and God won't have to yell at you.

Listen to Your Life

1. What noises disturb your spirit?

2. How do you listen to life through these noises?

3. What do you hear God saying to you through the noises?

Are you afraid to make a mistake?

I wanted to learn to play the guitar when I was a teenager. So I saved some money, bought a guitar and took lessons.

The guitar was beautiful, nothing extravagant, but it was at least a music store guitar and not a "dime store" guitar like some of my friends had. And it sounded beautiful when my instructor played it.

But it sounded a little different when I played it. I just couldn't make the music come out of the guitar that my teacher did. I practiced for hours, trying not to make mistakes, which meant that I'd get to the same place in a song and make the same mistake every time. My teacher said, "Everybody makes mistakes. That's the way we learn." All I learned was that my favorite group, the *Eagles*, would never discover me.

However, I finally learned to play *House of the Rising Sun* with no mistakes. (Had I known what it was about, I probably would have chosen another song, but it was easy and in my beginner book, okay?) But that was the only song I ever played, because I couldn't stand the mistakes of trying to learn another song. Eventually I put the guitar down, never picked it up again, and it's in my brother's basement today.

Since then I've learned that my teacher was right. The only people who aren't making mistakes are either dead or, like I did, quit trying. I've learned everybody makes mistakes and we can learn from them.

So learn from my mistake and keep trying to do whatever it is you're doing. You can, with God's help, grow past your mistakes and succeed.

Listen to Your Life
1. What have you tried to do that you haven't quite mastered?

2. What have you learned to do that you experienced lots of challenges learning, but eventually succeeded?

3. What is the difference between the two experiences? How did God make the difference?

Which do you like better—the sweet or the sour sauce?

One evening, our family had sweet and sour chicken for supper. I watched as our older daughter ate her third piece. I said to her, "You really like sweet and sour chicken, don't you?"

"Yes sir!" she said, "but I like the sweet part best. I told Mama I just wanted the sweet, not the sour part of the sauce."

Then my wife said, "But I explained to her that the sweet and the sour were together in the sauce. And that I couldn't separate them."

"That's okay," our daughter said as she ate that third piece, "I still like the sweet part best."

I'm like our daughter, aren't you? I like just the sweet part of life. No sour experiences for me! Nothing to make my tongue curl or my mouth pucker up. Or my eyes water. Or my insides knot-up. Or my feelings get hurt. Or my heart break. I want everything to go my way. That's the life for me! I like the sweet part best.

But as much as I like the sweet part best, my wife is right. As it is with sauce, so it is with life. It's just the way life is, isn't it? The sweet and the sour are together.

Just like my daughter, don't let the sour part of life's sauce keep you from enjoying the sweet. Keep eating at life's table until you're full.

And the next time your life turns sour, remember God mixes in the sweet so that you can stomach the sour.

Listen to Your Life

1. What's sour in your life?

2. What's sweet in your life?

3. What do you hear as you're listening to your life in the midst of the sweet and the sour?

Is there a crack in your relationship with God?

A culvert runs underneath our driveway. It connects two of our horse pastures, allowing the water to run from one pasture through the other one and into a little branch.

On either side of the driveway is a concrete-and-stone wall. I noticed last year that the top of the wall had a crack in it. I didn't think much about it until this year when I looked at it again.

Much to my surprise, the crack had grown much wider. In fact, it's so wide now that weeds and bushes are growing up through it. Even a little sweet gum tree sprouted up through it. It's so wide that I'm afraid that the wall is weakening.

So I cleared out the weeds and bushes and the little tree from the crack and filled it with concrete. I patched not just the surface of the crack, but poured the concrete down into the crack, filling it from where it starts to the top. Now the wall stands strong again.

The crack in that concrete-and-stone wall reminds me of how easy it is for a crack to grow in our relationships with God. It's easy for the weeds of hate and the bushes of chaos and the seedlings of separation to grow between God and us. We don't pay the crack much attention when it first starts, but later we see it when it gets wider.

Let God help you clear out the hate, chaos, and separation from the crack in your relationship. Let God fill it with unconditional love and grace. As you do, you can stand strong again.

Listen to Your Life

1. As you listen to your life, what life situation have you held back from God, thinking that you can handle it on your own?

2. What has been the result of this crack in your relationship with God?

3. When will you ask God to fill the crack with unconditional love and grace so that you can stand strong again?

There's no free lunch anymore, is there?

I traveled out of town to speak to a group about listening life. I got really hungry during the drive. I had hoped to make it to my hotel so that I could sit at a table and eat, but I was so hungry I decided to drive through a fast-food restaurant.

Stopping at the intercom, I ordered a sandwich and a medium soft drink, and then drove around to the window. I noticed my drink sitting at the window and it obviously wasn't a medium. That drink was huge—so large it looked like a bucket!

So I'm sitting there in my car at the window, and I'm thinking to myself, "I only ordered a medium drink and now she's fixed me that huge drink and is charging me for a huge drink. You just can't find good help these days."

Well at that very second, the young lady opens the window, smiles, and says to me, "Sir, I'm sorry we're out of medium cups. I gave you a large but only charged you for a medium."

And how do you think I felt? Yep, about that small. All I could stammer was, "Well, thanks!"

As I drove on down the road, feeding my face, I felt my spirit being fed as well. For I realized that God's like that—always trying to give us more of what we're hungry for than we asked for.

So maybe there is such a thing as a free lunch now. Accept God's free spiritual lunch as you listen to life today for what God has to say.

Listen to Your Life

1. When was the last time someone gave you something for free? What was your reaction?

2. What did you do later, in appreciation for the free gift?

3. What could God be trying to give you now?

Who says there aren't any nice people left in the world?

My wife was shopping with our two daughters. She was paying for their clothes and looked for her car keys in her purse. Guess where they were…that's right, she had done what we all do at some point in our lives—she locked her keys in the car.

She tried calling me on her mobile phone and couldn't reach only my voice mail because I was in a meeting or a session.

Not knowing exactly what to do next, she then explained to our daughters what had happened and that they'd be staying at the store a little longer than expected. The girls took it quite well, wanting to know if this meant they could shop some more. She then went out to the car just to make sure she couldn't get in.

When she came back into the store, a woman walked up and said, "I heard you say you locked your keys in your car. I called my husband—he works at a service station—and he'll be here in a minute to unlock your car."

My wife couldn't believe her ears! I mean, you only hear about these kinds of things happening on *Touched By an Angel*.

Well, the husband showed up in a few minutes, and unlocked my wife's car. As my wife reached into her purse and asked him how much she owed, he said, "There's no charge, ma'm." He wouldn't take a dollar for his services.

And who says there aren't any nice people left in the world?

Listen to Your Life

1. Does it ever seem to you like there aren't any nice people left in the world? Why or why not?

2. Do you believe God sends nice people in your times of need to overhear and respond with help? Why or why not? What examples can you offer?

3. What's the top story in the news today? How does that story compare with this story? Are there any nice people in the top news story? If so, what did they do? If not, wonder why?

What are you looking for?

L ots of dirt was being moved at the beach while we were on vacation. I mean tons of sand and dirt. A company was replenishing the beach front with sand from the ocean floor because a hurricane had eroded it. Pumping in tons of dirt from the ocean floor made the shallow shore water anything but clear.

Our younger daughter and I went down to check out the water. It was so muddy you couldn't see your feet or anything else even in the shallow water. It was so muddy that I said to our daughter, "Yuk! Look how dirty the ocean is."

And she said to me, "But Daddy, it looks like a chocolate ocean to me."

I looked down at the water again, and this time I saw it. The water really did look chocolate brown. And for a minute, I wanted to get down on my hands and knees and drink it up.

My daughter and I looked at the same ocean water, but with two entirely different perspectives. I saw, "Yuk!" She saw, "Yum!"

I guess what we see as we listen to our lives for what God has to say depends on our attitudes. If you're looking for a dirty ocean, that's what you'll see. If you're looking for a

41

chocolate ocean, then that's what you'll see.

You have a choice about what you look for in life—yuk or yum.

What are you looking for? Look for a chocolate ocean as you listen to life today for what God has to say.

Listen to Your Life

1. Think back to your last conversation with someone—a coworker, family member, or friend—about a situation. What did your remarks sound more like—yuk or yum?

2. What would it take for you to start looking for chocolate oceans as you listen to life?

3. How could God help transform your attitude?

Who empties the dishwasher at your home?

Who empties the dishwasher at your home? Not exactly one of those things everybody begs to do, is it? And yet everybody knows it needs emptying.

I can't take credit for this realization. My wife pointed it out to me one day. And in a burst of intellectual insight, I realized that yes, once again, she was right.

Why should she be the only one to empty the dishwasher? I mean everyone in our home could hear the clinging of dishes as my wife loaded them. Every one of us could hear them washing. All of us who walked by and looked at it could see that it was locked and loaded, just waiting to be opened and the dishes put away.

And it's not like my wife is the only one that benefits from the dishwasher's work. We all eat the same food cooked in the same pots and pans off of those same plates and use those same utensils.

But who emptied the dishwasher time after time? My wife.

And who ignored the dishwasher and walked on by? The rest of our family.

Who empties the dishwasher and puts away those plates and pots and pans at your home? And who ignores it and walks on by?

You and I face opportunities every day of our lives to do what needs to be done, to help out, just like with emptying the dishwasher.

God gives us these chances for us to do our best in helping one another.

So what will you do today? Empty the dishwasher or just walk on by?

Listen to life today for what God has to say about opportunities for you to help.

Listen to Your Life

1. Think about the seemingly menial tasks around your home. Who does them? And are they taken for granted for their doing?

2. Which of these tasks are you capable of doing? What would it take for you to do them occasionally?

3. Think about your spiritual life. What menial tasks does God do for you? Which of these tasks are you capable of helping God with?

Who built your nest?

We love watching birds on our farm. It doesn't matter whether it's a tiny hummingbird or a huge turkey, we just love watching birds.

We were all excited when a chickadee built a nest in the corner of our front porch. She built the nest very methodically over a period of several days. Besides the usual sticks and leaves, she brought horse hair from the pastures and stables on our farm. You could tell she was an experienced nest builder, very intentional about having the very best for her babies. She sat on her eggs continuously until finally the fledglings hatched out, got strong enough to fly, and took off. So the nest was empty…

…until one day another mother bird appeared on the nest; a mother bird of a completely different species laid her eggs in the nest that the first mother bird built. She did a little sprucing up, but her nest-building efforts in no way resembled the first mother bird's. Finally, her eggs hatched, and those baby birds grew strong enough to fly.

Now at first it seemed to me that the second mother bird was lazy, living off another bird's hard work until I realized that we're all like that second mother bird. God created this world—our nest—and we're just here for a short while.

45

About all we can really do is spruce up God's creations, doing our best not to destroy it, and using it to grow our families in healthy ways.

So when you see a bird today, remind yourself that God built that bird's nest, and yours.

Listen to Your Life

1. Remember a time when you benefited from someone else's work. Recall the many ways you received blessings from their labor.

2. Remember an experience in which someone else benefited from your work. What did you think/feel about that person benefiting from your work?

3. Reflect for a moment on what you appreciate most about the nest God built for you. What can you thank God for the most about your world?

Do you go with your first reaction?

I played golf recently with some friends and we had our own little tournament going. Everyone else had finished except my partner and I. As we came to the 18th hole, we led by a stroke.

Our drive made the fairway, but our second shot was in the rough. So we had an approach shot to the green, which wasn't that long but between the hole and us were some palm trees, pine trees, and bushes. My partner hit first and his ball sailed way over the green. So it was up to me to put the ball on the green.

The rest of the players were standing around the green. One of the guys started yelling at me, saying that I'd better pray before I hit this shot. He was trying to get inside of my head to make me nervous so I'd blow the shot and he would win.

Now my first reaction was to tell him to shut up, that if this was the only way he could win he didn't deserve to win. But I knew if I said that, he'd gotten what he wanted—he rattled me. And my shot was sure to be anywhere but on the green near the hole.

So I paused for a moment, took a deep breath, and instead of getting distracted with anger, just smiled, took out my 9 iron, and hit the ball to within ten feet of the hole where we putted out and won the tournament.

Do you go with your first reaction? You don't have to. Just smile and hit the ball. When you do, you're listening to life today for what God has to say.

Listen to Your Life

1. Describe a recent event when someone or something tried to rattle you. The event could have happened at work, home, or play.

2. Remember your first reaction. Did you express it? If so, how? If not, why?

3. What is God saying to you right now about that event and your reaction?

How do you spell hope?

When our older daughter was two, like most two-year olds, she was very intent on doing things for herself. "I do it, Daddy," she would tell me and then she would try and try to open the door, even though she could hardly reach the knob and the door weighed more than her, or make the puzzle piece fit upside down, or whatever else it was she was trying to do.

Sometimes, like all of us I guess, she wouldn't be able to do whatever she was attempting. But she would keep trying until she became so frustrated her words wouldn't come out right. In exasperation, she would say, "Hope me, Daddy" meaning to say, "Help me, Daddy."

Rather than take over for her and just do it myself, I replied, "Okay, I'll help you." Then I would say something like, "Let's pull on the door together" or "Let's turn the puzzle piece another way and try it." And without fail, she and I together, would do it.

I guess when you're frustrated there's not a lot of difference between help and hope, is there? When you're frustrated because you can't get the job done you need the hope that help is on the way. And when help finally arrives your soul fills up with hope that next time you can do it with the right kind of help.

Today, like our daughter, you'll probably try to do something that you think you can do on your own. "I do it, God," you'll say. But then after trying to the point of frustration, you'll realize that you could use the hope that God's help brings.

When that happens, just look up toward heaven and ask God to "hope you." Then listen to life today for what God has to say. And let God help you.

Listen to Your Life

1. When have you recently attempted to do something on your own and discovered you couldn't?

2. How did you feel? What were you thinking?

3. What kind of help from God would bring you help right now?

Do you ever have trouble resting in God?

When I was a college freshman, I rescued a white lab mouse from the biology lab. He had been a part of an experiment and was to be executed shortly.

I named him "Norman" after our college's president. I took Norman (the mouse) to my dorm room, then shopping. I bought him a nice, steel cage with food, water, wood shavings—everything a mouse could ever hope for—and a wheel.

Every night when I cut the lights out to go to sleep, Norman climbed in his wheel and started running. "Squeak, squeak, squeak," the wheel turned as Norman ran. It squeaked no matter what I put on the wheel—3-in-1 oil, WD40, vegetable oil.

Well you can imagine that sleeping while Norman squeaked running in his wheel was impossible. And no matter how hard I banged on the cage, knocking Norman out of the wheel, very shortly he was back in it, running again. The only way I ever got any sleep was to take the wheel out of the cage.

Do you ever have trouble resting in God?

Could it be the squeaky wheel in your spirit?

Are you like Norman, running, creating noise in your own spirit, preventing you from resting in God?

Or, is there a squeaky wheel at work or in your marriage that disrupts your spirit's relaxing in God's?

Whatever its source, take the squeaky wheel out of your spirit, and listen to life today for what God has to say. And enjoy the rest in God.

Listen to Your Life

1. What squeaks in your spirit? It could be something you do or someone else does at work or home.

2. How do you deal with the squeak? What emotions do you spray it with? How often do you bang on it?

3. How can you more effectively treat the squeak in your spirit? How can you rest in God?

What do you want the most?

A survey conducted for a Fortune 100 financial services company looked at what workers want most from their employers. It found that the number one desire, that is what workers want most from their bosses, is personal feedback. The trends behind this desire include the fact that more workers are involved in decision-making with increased responsibility and fewer guarantees of job security.

Or, as one worker put it, "The feeling that someone cares far outweighs a money value." What workers want most from their bosses is to know someone cares.

I wouldn't have thought that most workers wanted care from their bosses, would you? Wouldn't you think that most employees are more concerned with financial raises or increased benefits or more vacation time? I would.

But the survey says employees want personal feedback of such a nature that they know someone cares.

Maybe work then is more a matter of the heart beat than the bottom line. Maybe even work relationships can bring us a spiritual satisfaction. Maybe, just maybe, if we listen to life carefully God can speak to us at work.

What do you want the most? Not just from your boss, but from others?

What do you want the most from God?

If we could survey God, I imagine we'd discover that what God most wants to give us is what we most want to receive—care.

So get what you want most and what God wants to give most—care—by listening to life today for what God has to say especially at work.

Listen to Your Life

1. What do you want the most from your employer? Or, if you're an employer, what do you want the most from your employees?

2. How do you know when someone cares about you?

3. In what ways does God care for you?

Why do you do what you do?

I was on vacation recently and went to the grocery store early one morning. It was our first morning there so we needed some breakfast food.

I stood in the check out line with my milk and cereal and overheard a conversation between the woman in line ahead of me and the cashier. It seems the woman wanted to cash a check while buying the milk, but the cashier didn't want to do it. A discussion followed. There was a disagreement. So the manager got involved and told the woman there was a bank down the street. The woman said her baby needed some milk now and the bank didn't open for another hour.

In the mean time, the cashier started checking my groceries and before she totaled it up, I told her, "Put that woman's milk on my bill."

The cashier looked at me like I was crazy and said, "Why do you wanna do that?"

"Because her baby needs it," I said.

"Oh," she said, smiled, and totaled my groceries.

As I drove back to the beach house, I wondered what I should have said when the cashier asked me, "Why do you wanna do that?" Should I have said something more theologically sound like, "Because God cares about this woman and her baby" or something like that.

But then I remembered the cashier's smile when I told her why. And I decided that my buying the woman's milk because her baby needed it said enough about why I did what I did.

Why do you do what you do?

As you listen to life today, you'll hear God giving you opportunities to let your actions say just about everything that needs to be said. Let your actions and a few words explain to others why you do what you do.

Listen to Your Life

1. What would you have said to the cashier?

2. Which speaks louder—your actions or your words?

3. Have you thought lately about why you do what you do?

What's on your refrigerator?

Sometimes I think that the only reason we have a refrigerator in our home is to display the important artwork and school papers our daughters bring home. Of course, this means that the front and sides of our refrigerator are pretty full. In fact, some days we have to move the latest masterpiece just to find the handle to open the door.

Recently our younger daughter brought home yet another artistic wonderment to put on our refrigerator. "Daddy, where would you like me to put this on the refrigerator?" she asked me.

I told her, "Honey, there's no room on the refrigerator for anything else."

She looked at me as only she can—you know, the "I can't believe you said that" look—hands on hips, and said, "Daddy, this is important. I want it on the refrigerator."

Well, you know what I did. That's right—I moved around the stuff on the refrigerator and made room for her latest creation.

When I had finished, she said, "Now, isn't that better?"

And immediately I realized how important putting the new picture on the refrigerator was to her. You see, I wasn't just putting any picture up. This picture was important because it represented her. She felt valued and loved—important to me—because her picture was put up on the refrigerator.

Some things in life are really important, aren't they?

If God has a refrigerator in heaven, I bet your picture is on it. You are very important to God. Just listen to life today for what God has to say about how important you are.

Listen to Your Life

1. Where did your parents put up your artwork?

2. What makes you feel important to others?

3. What life event recently reminded you how important you are to God?

What's the best gift you've ever received?

Recently, I was in our home's basement, looking through some old albums I have. I found a copy of *Poems, Prayers, and Promises* by John Denver and remembered the story of that album.

When I was a teenager, John Denver was really popular and this was his newest album. I wanted that album and how. I distinctly remember standing in the record store, staring at that album, convincing myself that my mother would love it as much as I did and if she didn't, well, maybe, she'd let me "borrow" it. (What I really hoped was that she wouldn't love it as much as I did and just give it to me.) So I gave it as a Christmas gift to her. She did let me "borrow" it and that's why the album is now in a box in my basement.

I kind of missed the spirit of giving, don't you think?

I acted nothing like my loving wife who, knowing that I always ask for practical gifts like hedge clippers, bought me a Christmas gift I absolutely adore to this day: a Three Stooges baseball cap. It's great—something I would have never bought for myself. And she doesn't even like the Three Stooges or wear baseball caps.

More like my wife than me, God loves you so much that God unselfishly gives you the gift of today, the present—something you can't buy for yourself. God doesn't give you this present with the expectation of "borrowing" it back from you. God unconditionally offers you today as a no-strings attached gift of love.

So unwrap the present and enjoy this day that God gives you in love.

Listen to Your Life

1. Have you ever given someone a gift that you really wanted? What was it? Who was it?

2. Have you ever received a gift from someone that was just perfect for you? What was it? Who was it?

3. As you unwrap this moment—as you read this—what is God giving you?

Do you ever feel like you're missing something?

A friend told me about camping out with a Boy Scout troop in a game preserve. Boys being boys, after they set up their tents and campsites, they went running through the game preserve trails, kind of like a herd of buffalo on a prairie plain. They were hooping and hollering, running and racing.

Well, my friend watched all of this activity with a lot of interest. The next morning after breakfast, he asked the boys to join him to go down the trail again. Now of course the boys thought they'd get to do their buffalo act again. So they took off, hooping and hollering, running and racing again.

But this time, my friend asked the boys not to run, and instead to get down on their hands and knees and crawl the trail, looking for anything they could find of interest. At first the boys thought he was crazy, but after a few minutes of crawling, they discovered what he was after. This time, by crawling, they saw things they had missed the first time through—tiny flowers and forest creatures, moss growing on the north side of trees, and other such created wonders.

After a little while of crawling and observing, he invited them to sit down and talk about what they saw. When they finished, he asked, "Now did you see any of these things your

61

first time down the trail?"

You know their answer—of course they didn't.

Then why do we race through life like a herd of buffalo and miss so much of what God wants us to experience? Why do we not do life more often on our knees?

Do your life trail differently today. Slow down your pace, get on your knees, and listen to life today for what God has to say. You'll be amazed by what you're missing!

Listen to Your Life

1. How would you describe your daily pace down life's trail—running and racing or crawling and considering?

2. What are the benefits and the liabilities to your spirit of your chosen pace?

3. At which pace do you better experience God? What can you do to live more in that pace?

Need a second chance?

L ast year, I painted the board fencing on our farm. I bought a five-gallon bucket of paint and lugged it up and down the fence line as I smeared it with my four-inch brush.

Section by section, I painted one side of the fence, and then went to the other side. At one section, there wasn't a gate close by and I really didn't want to carry that heavy bucket up the hill to the gate. So I came up with the brilliant idea of lifting the bucket up over the fence, putting it down on the other side, and then climbing over the fence myself. Sounds easy enough, right?

Well, I got the heavy bucket over the top board of the fence, but then as it got closer to the ground on the other side and as I stretched further and further to let it down, I tipped and spilled it on the ground. I wasn't very pleased with myself. (Okay, I was angry.)

So I climbed over the fence, and looked at the mess I'd made, wondering why I couldn't have held the bucket more firmly until it touched the ground. Just then, from my new perspective on the other side of the fence, I noticed that the bottom of the fence was high enough for me to have slid the bucket under the fence instead of lifting it over.

Well, you can imagine what I was thinking—"I wish I had

a second chance to do that over."

Do you ever wish for a second chance? You do something. It doesn't turn out the way you wanted. You get a new perspective on it, and realize what you should have done. Then you want a second chance.

God is the God of second chances. God gives us all the second chances we need in life. So take a chance on God, even a second chance today.

Listen to Your Life

1. What have you done lately that you wish you could do differently?

2. What new perspective helped you see the situation differently?

3. What second chance will you ask God for today?

How do you treat people who are different from you?

Last spring we had some termites flying around our house and that sort of got our attention. I called around to find someone who'd come out and treat our house. I found someone, he came out, and drilled holes and sprayed chemicals all day. If you've ever had your house treated, you know that afterwards—well, there's no polite way to say this—your house just stinks for a while.

After coming home from school, our younger daughter walked in the house and immediately wanted to know what the smell was all about in our house. "What did you do?" she asked. I told we'd had the house treated for termites.

A little while later I went upstairs to her bedroom. The door was shut so I politely knocked. She said, "Come in" which I did. Her room smelled like one of those bath products and perfume stores. I immediately wanted to know what the smell was all about. I asked, "What did you do?"

And she said, "I treated my room for me."

When you meet someone that gets your attention by being different from you, how do you treat that person?

Do you spray for him, treating him with a stink? Or do you treat her like you want to be treated?

Who do you treat your life's room for?
And what treatment does God want you to offer?

Listen to Your Life

1. Recall the last event in which you ran into someone really different from you? How did you react?

2. If you gave your reaction the name of a smell, what flavor or scent would it be?

3. What treatment does God want you to offer that person?

Are you plugged in?

M y secretary was out of the office one day. We had a volunteer take her place. Now this volunteer secretary is a wonderful, kind person, the type who's always thinking of others. The kind of woman who asks what you like and how you like it, then knocks herself out to provide it.

Well, she knew how much I love coffee. So she decided to make me some coffee before I came in to the office. She's not a coffee drinker herself, but she measured out the coffee carefully, filled the percolator with water, and thought she had everything perfect so that I could just walk in and pour myself a cup.

You can imagine when I came in and didn't say anything about smelling perked coffee, she was wondering what was wrong with me. She offered all sorts of subtle hints, none of which I picked up on. So then she escorted me to the break room, showed me the percolator and wanted to know what was wrong with me. Why couldn't I smell the coffee and be impressed?

As best I could, I politely thanked her for making the coffee and assured her how much I appreciated it, but before I enjoyed her coffee…I'd better plug in the percolator.

Do you ever feel like you've done everything right to please

God and wonder why nobody notices? And even wonder why God doesn't notice?

It's not a matter of doing the right things in life. It's more a matter of being connected to the Power Source.

So when you think you've done everything right and not gotten the results you wanted, look inside and make sure your spirit is plugged into God's Spirit. Then listen to life today for what God has to say.

Listen to Your Life

1. Remember a recent occasion when you thought you had done everything right only to discover later that you had not.

2. How did you feel? What did you think?

3. How could plugging your spirit into God's Spirit have made a difference in this situation?

Who's your friend?

It was spring, a beautiful time of year on our farm. Trees were budding, chasing the winter gray away. Showers were plentiful. And our grass seemed like it was growing in six-inch spurts.

My wife and I mowed every week until our lawn mower broke. The repair shop said it would take at least a couple of weeks to fix it. During those two weeks, our grass would be knee-high before we could mow it again.

Now this wasn't a crisis situation, just an inconvenience, but you know how it is—life is full of inconveniences and they pile up sometimes. Our mower breaking was just one more thing to go wrong.

So we fretted about it. We fretted so much that we even mentioned to some friends about the grass growing so much and the lawnmower being broken and we didn't know what we were going to do so we guessed we'd just have to pay somebody an exorbitant amount of money to cut it and then still have to pay to have the mower fixed. (I know—we were whining.)

Well the next weekend, guess who showed up at our home and mowed our yard? That's right—our friends. Just when we needed it they came through for us—doing for us what we couldn't do for ourselves.

God is like our friends. God comes through for us, doing for us what we can't do for ourselves. So today when you run into an inconvenience or a crisis and even when you're whining about it, just remember—God is about to come through for you.

Listen to Your Life
1. How have you been inconvenienced recently?

2. What was your reaction to the inconvenience?

3. Reflecting on the experience, how did God come through for you?

What time is it?

A listener/reader of *Listen to Life with Dr. Joey Faucette* emailed me, saying she recently had visited her daughter and family. During the visit, the daughter needed to run an errand so the proud grandmother offered to stay home with the preschool-aged grandson. (You know how most grandmothers are—"I never get to see him enough.")

Well, shortly after she left, the preschooler started missing his Mommy. "I want my Mommy," he said to his grandmother.

"Mommy will be home soon," the grandmother reassured him. "In the meantime, would you like for me to read one of your books to you?" she asked.

The little fellow looked at his grandmother strangely, but agreed and hopped up on the couch next to her.

After the grandmother had read for a while, she felt him snuggle up next to her. Oh, what joy it brought to her heart to be spending time with her dear darling grandson.

As he snuggled up even closer, he said to his grandmother, "This isn't a mean time. This is a good time."

There are many "meantime's" in life, aren't there? Times when the people we get security and affection from leave us for a while. And some times when it seems like God leaves us for a while.

What time is it for you in your life right now? A mean time? Or, a good time? Even when the time seems mean, God can make it good. God hasn't really gone anywhere. Just snuggle up and listen to life today for what God has to say. And you'll find God right beside you...and you can say, "This is a good time."

Listen to Your Life

1. When have you felt abandoned?

2. Who did God send to bring you what you needed?

3. Who do you know that's living in a "meantime" right now? Is God nudging you to take a "good time" to that person?

What is God's plan for your life?

We sat there, eating lunch together, and talking. He told me about when his little girl died. Then he told me about the baby his wife miscarried a month before the due date.

I sat there thinking about our two healthy, vibrant, and alive girls. Both of them the proverbial apples of our eyes. Both of them enjoying life to the fullest and bringing great joy to my wife and me in the process. Frankly, I couldn't imagine a day without them both. And I didn't want to even consider what life would be like without either of them.

So I told my friend, "I can't tell you I know how you feel. I haven't been where you are."

"Thank you," he said. "It drove me crazy when someone said they knew how I felt. They hadn't been where I was. And then someone else told me it was God's plan for my babies to die. That couldn't be God's plan for their lives or my life, could it?"

I knew he was listening to every word I was about to say. This was his life and he was trying to make sense of it. So I paused, breathed a prayer, and then told him, "No, it's not God's plan for little girls to suffer and die, but it is God's plan to take care of their daddy."

I don't know how you feel today, because I'm not where you are, but whatever is going on with you that is really driving you crazy, remember—it's God's plan to care of you. Just pause, breathe a prayer, and then listen to life today for what God has to say. God will take care of you.

Listen to Your Life

1. Where are you in life today? What's driving you crazy?

2. What are other people telling you that just doesn't make sense to you?

3. Close your eyes for a moment and pause. Breathe a prayer. Then listen to your life. What is God saying about taking care of you?

Are you looking for something familiar?

Our family was driving home from the beach and it was lunchtime. Our daughters would have loved another fast food meal with a useless toy in it. My wife would have loved to eat some more crab legs. But it was my turn to choose the restaurant and I was looking for something familiar, like my grandmother used to fix—a home-cooked meal.

I've learned through the years that you just can't find "grandma's cooking" restaurants on an interstate exit. So I detoured from the interstate and found "The Coffee Shop." There were no neon or "meal deal" posters in the windows. We peeked in the front door and somebody's grandma greeted us and said, "Hi! Ya'll come on in. Would you like to eat the buffet?"

"Uh, yes ma'am," I said.

"Well, fix your plate and have a seat."

"Yes, ma'am!" I said. It was like talking to my own grandmother.

And the place smelled a lot like my grandmother's kitchen. As I sat down in the booth with my family, there was something familiar about that meal. Even though I never had been in that place I felt like I had. I felt like I was at home.

I guess we're all looking for something familiar what with

the fast pace of change today. Daily, we're bombarded by news of change—genetic cloning, stem cell research, international space stations, the stock market, and webcasting. Some days, wouldn't you just love some spiritual familiarity? A place where your spirit can rest, relax, and be fed something familiar?

I've learned through the years that you can't find "soul food" on an interstate exit. Get off the interstate of your life, out of the fast lane, and see where God leads you. You may be surprised at how good the familiar can be.

Listen to Your Life

1. What have you fed your spirit lately—fast food or soul food?

2. How nourished is your spirit by this diet?

3. What could you order from God's menu that's familiar to you, i.e., that your spirit has been nourished with before?

What feeds your soul?

A couple of years ago, I planted eight rose bushes in a bed. Near the bed were some walnut trees.

The rose bushes didn't grow very well, but I thought it was because it was their first season and they needed time to mature. I removed a couple of the walnut trees, thinking that might help by allowing more sunlight to get to the roses. And I guess it did, but the roses still didn't grow a lot.

So I decided to find out why. What I discovered was that walnut trees have root systems that take most of the nutrients out of the soil surrounding them. Also, walnut trees, through their shed leaves and the husks protecting the fallen nuts, give off some form of acid, which kills other plants around them.

All of this means that my roses couldn't grow well because I didn't know that the walnut trees had taken all the normal nourishment out of the soil. So I started feeding the roses twice as often as recommended and they grew and bloomed much better.

Do you ever feel like your spirit's not growing very well? Like you want to bloom more than you are, but you just lack something? And you don't know what it is?

You know, there are lots of walnut trees in life—situations

or people that want to nourish themselves and take away your spirit's nourishment. When your spirit's not growing well, look around, discover what's stealing your spiritual nourishment, and remove those things.

Then feed your soul some extra spirit from God—twice the recommended amount—by listening to life today for what God has to say.

Listen to Your Life

1. How do you know when your spirit is or isn't growing well?

2. What steals your spiritual nourishment at work? In your family? In other relationships?

3. How can God help you remove these spiritually toxic things?

Are you ready to ride?

It was one of the best weeks of my young life. I was old enough to get my first pair of bell-bottom blue jeans and my first full-sized bicycle. Man, I was so cool! (It was the 60's, okay?) Of course, I just had to wear those bell-bottom blue jeans while riding my adult-sized bike up and down our street. You see, there was a girl involved whom I desperately wanted to impress. Not exactly the girl next door. More like the girl down the street. And I hoped she would be watching out of her window while I rode in front of her house. Yep, I was so cool…

…until my bell-bottom wrapped around the chain on my bike, caught, flipped me over the handle bars, and onto the pavement. The bent bike landed on top of me, my jeans ripped, and my knee, elbow, and hand were all bleeding. (Thank goodness it didn't happen in front of her house!)

The good news is my parents bought me some more jeans and I learned never to wear bell-bottoms while riding a bike. The bad news is I've got a scar on my knee today to remind me of that experience. But you know, that incident didn't keep me off my bike. I did ride again.

I'll bet you have some scars and not just on a knee or elbow either. Maybe your heart is scarred from getting caught in a relationship and thrown off by someone. Or, maybe your heart is scarred from some childhood incident in your home. Or, maybe your scar is in your spirit from some incident that you blame God for. These scars are the bad news.

The good news is your scars can remind you of danger, but you don't have to let those painful memories keep you from life. You can ride again while you listen to life today for what God has to say.

Listen to Your Life

1. Where's your scar?

2. How did you get it?

3. How can God heal you and help you ride again?

How's your attitude?

A friend of mine went to the doctor, had some tests, and was told that her bone density was extremely low. Her prognosis was that she could never recover her bone density, that she had better slow down her pace as she walked each morning, and be very careful not to fall.

"I was ready for the nursing home when the doctor told me that," she said. In fact, she got a little blue about that prognosis. She's a very active person who embraces life with a fullness and energy rare among women her age. She was afraid that her lifestyle would have to change dramatically. So she began feeling sorry for herself...

...until she went shopping and saw a man who was missing an arm. "I'll bet he'd love to have my bone density," she thought.

Then she saw a woman in a wheelchair who obviously couldn't move her legs. "I'll bet she'd love to have my bone density," she thought again.

Suddenly, it began to dawn on my friend that maybe her prognosis wasn't the death sentence she thought it was. So she quit her pity party and decided to go on living.

I'm like my friend sometimes, aren't you? Something happens or someone makes a remark that reminds us of our limitations. And we start feeling sorry for ourselves.

The next time you throw a pity party for yourself over some situation, remember my friend. Your situation really could be worse. And remember that God is with you, helping you adjust your attitude so that you too can go on living and listening to life today for what God has to say.

Listen to Your Life

1. Recall something that happened to you recently or a remark someone made to you that reminded you of your limitations. How did you feel? What did you think? Did you throw a pity party for yourself?

2. How did you decide the pity party was over?

3. What can God say to you today to adjust your attitude about life?

What do you need to let out?

Our younger daughter really doesn't like to get up in front of a crowd. She is introverted and prefers small groups to large crowds. So it was a big deal for her when she sang in the elementary school chorus at a Parents-Teachers Organization (PTO) meeting of several hundred people.

Of course she did great, knowing all the lyrics and following her director closely. Afterwards, as we drove home and talked, she was so relieved that the whole thing was over.

"How did you feel?" I asked her.

"My stomach felt funny when I was up on the stage," she said.

I told her, "Oh, those were butterflies."

"How did butterflies get in my stomach?" she asked.

"They weren't really butterflies," I explained. "It just felt like butterflies flying around your stomach."

"Well," she said, "I wish I had known they were butterflies because I would have opened my mouth and let them out."

Like our daughter, sometimes in life we wish we had known so we could let something out.

What is in your spirit that you need to let out? Something you've done in the past? Or, something someone did to you? Or, some anxiety over what could happen?

Just open your spirit today and let it out whatever it is. Then keep your spirit open and listen to life today for what God has to say about your spiritual butterflies.

Listen to Your Life

1. What's fluttering around inside of your spirit, making you nervous or keeping you from listening to life? Just as butterflies have names, give your spiritual butterfly a name.

2. Now that you've given it a name, open your spirit to God and let your spiritual butterfly out. Ask God to remove it from you.

3. With your spiritual butterfly releasing, listen for what God says to you. What do you hear?

How long can you hold your breath?

How long can you hold your breath? A couple of minutes? An hour? A day? A month?

At best you can hold your breath only for a few minutes. Then your body starts screaming for more oxygen. It's used up everything you've stored in your lungs. You have to breathe again or die.

Well, if you can hold your breath only for a few minutes, how much can you eat in one meal? Enough food to last you all day? What about all week? Maybe all month?

At best you can only eat enough in one meal to last you for a day, maybe two. But after that your body starts screaming for more food. It's used up all the energy you've stored. You have to eat again or die.

We have to breathe and eat often, don't we? We regularly have to renew our body's resources if we want to live.

Just like with our breathing and eating, we have to take in God's grace often, daily, just to make it through today. We can't expect to make it on what we can take in of God's grace for one hour of one day in one week. As we live, our supply of God's grace is depleted by the daily tasks of making a living, being family, and all the other activities we find necessary. We need God's grace every day so that we can spiritually live.

God knows we need grace to survive and thrive. That's why God speaks to us in so many ways every day, trying to let us know how loved we are.

So breathe deeply, eat well, and take in God's grace by listening to life today for what God has to say.

Listen to Your Life

1. How often do you take in God's grace?

2. What does God say to you through your events and activities, feelings and thoughts that best feeds your spirit grace?

3. Where and when can you breathe in and be fed God's grace more often?

How do you pray?

When she was younger, our first-born daughter began her prayers the same way every night: "Dear God, thank you for the beautiful day it'll be tomorrow."

You know, it takes a great deal of faith to pray those words. Just think about it for a minute.

It takes faith because many of us are more interested in what God can do for us tomorrow instead of giving thanks ahead of time for whatever comes our way tomorrow. I guess our need to control life gets in the way of our trusting God enough to give thanks for what God wants to do with tomorrow. As if we know more about tomorrow than God, eh?

It takes faith because regardless of the weather forecast, our daughter's tomorrow will be beautiful. She measures the beauty of her tomorrow not in frontal systems, jet streams, or barometric pressure, but family systems, streams of unconditional love, and pressure measured in hugs. That's how she sees life's beauty coming to her tomorrow.

It takes faith because she trusts God to bring tomorrow and see her through it, come what may. For her, that trust is the bottom-line of her daily living. Sure, something could go wrong. She could fall and skin her knee on the playground. Or, a classmate could take a crayon. Or, she could spill juice on her clothes. Nonetheless, she trusts God to make tomorrow beautiful.

So how do you pray? Try "Dear God, thank you for the beautiful day it'll be tomorrow" and feel your faith grow as you listen to life today for what God has to say.

Listen to Your Life

1. Remember your last prayer. What did you say to God?

2. In that prayer, did you ask God for something more than you thanked God?

3. What would happen to your faith if you prayed daily, "Dear God, thank you for the beautiful day it'll be tomorrow"?

What are you sharing?

A friend of mine told me a story about Riley Barnett.

Riley Barnett lived in the Appalachian Mountains in a tarpaper shack with no running water or any other conveniences we have. A developer built an affluent neighborhood around Riley's shack, but Riley wouldn't sell his small plot of land. Had he sold the land, Riley would have had plenty of money. But Riley Barnett loved his place and the tarpaper shack in which he lived.

You see, he grew a garden every year on that land. Between the garden, $28 a month in food stamps, and neighbors giving him clothes and other goods, Riley managed to live.

But Riley Barnett did more than just manage to live. Every Saturday, he would ask my friend to drive him around. This trip was not just one of those Saturday-go-to-town trips. Instead, Riley took vegetables from his garden and clothes and canned goods the neighbors gave him on his trip. He went door-to-door, giving them to people who lived in the city's projects and slums.

Riley Barnett, a man most people thought had nothing, shared something out of his nothing. Riley Barnett, a man most people thought eccentric, listened to life each day for what God had to say.

I don't know too many Riley Barnett's, do you? Most of us listen to life and hear only the Madison Avenue pitch of "bigger is better" and "more is best."

Today when you catch yourself wanting something else, think about Riley Barnett who shared something out of his nothing. And see if you can share something out of your everything.

Listen to Your Life

1. What do you think Riley Barnett heard God saying that most of us ignore?

2. When was the last time you cleaned out your attic or basement or went through your closet and pulled out clothes you never wear and gave them away?

3. Listen to life today for what God says to you about sharing something out of your everything. Listen for opportunities for you to give something away and seize the moment through a spontaneous act of giving.

Are you at home?

O ur daughters were picking blueberries on our farm one evening. Suddenly a big yellow Labrador Retriever walked up, wagging his tail, acting like he wanted some blueberries. He was so big that our younger daughter started crying, thinking he might want some of her, also. Our older daughter talked softly to the dog. The two of them fed him a few blueberries, petted him on the head, and called my wife.

The next thing I knew my wife was giving him a tick and flea bath, he'd swallowed a bowl of cat food, and was asleep on the back porch. The next day he was named "Charles Anthony Faucette"—nicknamed "Charlie"—and with that, he was at home. And he's acted like he's at home since then.

Recently, as I was picking blueberries and remembering Charlie's arrival, I started thinking about how he has it made at home. I mean he just showed up one day and now all of his needs are taken care of. Not only is he fed daily, our younger daughter plays with him every afternoon. Our older daughter pets him and rubs his back every time she walks by him. He's afraid of thunderstorms so we leave the garage door open for him to take shelter in a storm. Even our cats, Maybelle and Norman, rub on him and play with him.

But then I thought about how we all have it made at home like Charlie. We just show up in this world and God gives us a name and everything we need. All we have to do is act like we're at home in life...which we do when we listen to life today for what God has to say.

Listen to Your Life

1. Think about how you just showed up one day—were born—and how your needs were met by your family. What did they do for you that you couldn't do for yourself?

2. How can you act like you're home in life?

3. What does God provide for you that you can't provide for yourself?

Need a blessing?

I got an email from a friend, reminding me that I had spent some time coaching her husband about a job change he felt God wanted him to make. At the time, he worked as a state policeman, but what he really wanted to do was to start his own trucking company. So we worked together on a transition plan for him, praying for God to guide him and give him wisdom as he planned.

I moved from the area and had not heard how his plans were progressing until her email came. She went on to tell me that he took the final step in the process recently—buying a truck, quitting his law enforcement job, and going on the road.

While on his very first run as a self-employed, full-time truck driver, he was surfing radio stations, listening to pass the time. He tuned in a station and a voice caught his attention.

"I know that voice," he said.

It was my voice. The radio station he tuned in was playing our syndicated radio program, *Listen to Life with Dr. Joey Faucette.*

He took it as God's blessing on his decision.

Life is like that sometimes, isn't it? We don't always know or see the positive effects we can have on someone else's life.

We just do the best we can to guide people into listening to their lives for what God has to say. Then we trust God to know and take care of the details with them.

So Alan, wherever you are on the road today—who knows, you may be reading this book—keep on trucking by listening to life today for what God has to say.

Listen to Your Life

1. Remember a time when something happened to you that could have been a coincidence, but you understood it as providence.

2. How was that event a part of God's plan for your life?

3. What blessing should you ask God for today? As you ask, listen for God's response.

What do you think grace looks like?

When I was a little boy, I loved playing baseball. I played third base for the Little League White Sox team. Brooks Robinson was my third-base idol. My plans were for him to play for the Orioles until I grew up and came and take his place at the "hot box."

Also, I batted clean up. Henry Aaron was my hero here. He could make the ball fly out of any park. I dreamed of meeting him one day.

I still remember one game when I had a great game at the plate with several base hits, driving in some runs. I came to bat with two outs, runners on base. Visions of "Hammerin' Hank" ran through my mind.

But the other team changed pitchers, putting in their best one—a big guy with a fastball that sizzled as it popped into the catcher's mitt.

I stepped into the batter's box, ready to get a base hit. But after three pitches, the umpire screamed, "Strike 3, you're out!"

I couldn't believe it. I had struck out.

I remember walking back to the dugout, my eyes filling with tears of disappointment. My coach, Ed Shackleford, met me halfway with the words, "It's all right, Joey. You'll get 'em next time."

To me, grace looks like my coach telling me "It's all right. You'll get 'em next time." He believed that there would be a next time. I couldn't see beyond my failure in the moment. He believed that not only would there be a next time, but that I would get a hit. I didn't think I would ever hit the ball again. He believed in me and that I would be all right. And because he believed, I could, too.

What do you think grace looks like?

Listen to Your Life

1. Remember a time from your childhood when someone showed you grace by believing in you when you didn't believe in yourself.

2. Ask God to give you an opportunity to share your story with a friend or family member today. Ask God who you should look for.

3. What does God's grace look like to you?

What attracts you?

It's a big world out there. Especially when you're a child.

So when our younger daughter came home from second grade one day all excited about a science experiment, I listened carefully.

"Daddy, it was so cool," she said. "Did you know that a magnet can pick up a nail through a glass jar?"

"Really?" I said.

"It sure can. The magnet picks up the nail through the side of the jar but it won't pick up the jar," she said.

"Now why is that?" I said.

"Because the nail is attracted to the magnet and the glass isn't."

"What do you mean 'attracted'?" I said.

"That means the nail wants to come to the magnet and the glass doesn't," she explained. "That's why the magnet can pick up the nail."

What attracts you? What do you want to come to?

There is within your spirit an attraction to God. You want to come to God.

Granted, there are lots of glass jars and other things that aren't attracted to God in life. Sometimes, these other things get in between God and us. And we find it more challenging to experience God's pull in our spirits.

God's spiritual magnet can pick you up in life, no matter what is between you and God. God's magnet pulls you to God through all circumstances of life.

So go to God when you feel that tug in your spirit. Enjoy your attraction to God by listening to life today for what God has to say.

Listen to Your Life

1. It's a big world out there. Even when you're an adult. What has fascinated you about life recently?

2. When have you felt God's spiritual magnet pulling on your spirit lately?

3. Listening to life today for what God has to say is one way of experiencing your spiritual attraction to God. What are other ways?

How much of life are you soaking up?

If you put a sponge under running water, within a few minutes it's saturated, isn't it? It won't hold any more water.

But what if you left the sponge under the running water for five more minutes? Would it hold any more?

But what if you left the sponge under the running water for a whole day? Would it hold any more?

How about if you left it under the running water for a whole week? Would it hold any more?

What would you have to do for the sponge to hold more water?

You'd have to squeeze it out, right? Then and only then can the sponge hold more water.

God made us like a sponge. We can only soak up more of life when we squeeze our lives and give away to someone else what we've received from God. When we give away what God's given us, then and only then can God give us more of the beautiful wonder of life.

So how much of life are you soaking up?

Give your life a squeeze and give away what God's given you.

If you're not sure what to give away or where to give it, ask God, then listen to your life today for what God has to say about these opportunities to give yourself a squeeze.

Listen to Your Life

1. Remember an event in your life when you were squeezed by a situation—maybe it wasn't very pleasant—and you were amazed by how much more of life you soaked up.

2. What is something God has given you—spiritually or otherwise—that you can give away?

3. How can you squeeze yourself today?

Do you understand how much God loves you?

My wife has a registered quarter horse that she absolutely loves. "Seeker" is a tall and lean sorrel mare with a real sweet disposition. She and my wife do very well together. All of which means my wife is very careful about who she lets work on her horse when it's time for the vet or the farrior.

I was at the horse barn with her when the farrior showed up to shoe her horse. I knew he must be great at what he does or he wouldn't be at our farm. So I watched him very closely to see why he's the best.

Here's what I noticed. He took his time with Seeker, getting to know her and giving her an opportunity to know him. When the time seemed right, he didn't just pick up any horseshoe out of his rack and throw it on her hoof. Instead, he carefully measured her hoof, took the shoe to the anvil and banged it into shape, measured it again against her hoof, banged it some more; took it over to the grinder, smoothed off some rough edges, then measured it some more.

He patiently worked that shoe into the just-right shape for Seeker's hoof until finally, when he was satisfied that it fit perfectly, he nailed it in place. It wasn't until he was satisfied with the fit that he put it in place.

He finished up by trimming off the ends of the nails. Then he sealed the hoof.

Now do you understand why my wife has him as her farrior? He gives that same fine attention to detail to every horse he shoes.

Like my wife's farrior, God gives your life the same fine attention to detail. God works your life with you until the circumstances in your life fit perfectly. Only when God is satisfied does your life fit. And God seals your life with unconditional love.

Now do you understand how much God loves you?

Listen to Your Life

1. What's happened in your life recently that "fit" you just right?

2. How does that event relate to you how much God loves you?

3. When do you expect that to happen again?

Who is someone that made a great impression on you?

I remember Charlotte Forrest. She taught me when I was in the Primary Department in my church's Sunday School. She had a huge impact on my spiritual life, but not just at church.

Later in my life, she was also my tenth grade geometry teacher. I watched her daily in that classroom, remembering what she said in my Primary class and checking her out to see if she lived what she taught. And she did.

Some years ago, I received a letter from Mrs. Forrest complimenting me on an article I wrote. She signed her letter, "Charlotte Forrest, Mathematics, THS" (Tarboro High School).

I wrote her back, thanking her for her kind words. I told her that while I remembered her as my geometry teacher, my far stronger memories were of her showing me her faith in geometry class. I signed my letter, "Joey Faucette, attempted mathematics, learned faith."

God sends people like Charlotte Forrest to all of us. You had someone like her who made a great and positive impression on you.

Like you, I'm very grateful for the Charlotte Forrest's of

the world who give of themselves and live out of a consistent spirituality. But do you ever wonder who the next Charlotte Forrest will be? Who God will send to you to make another great impression?

God still sends Charlotte Forrests to all of us which means God still is calling Charlotte Forrests. Could you be a Charlotte Forrest to someone?

Sure you can. Just listen to life for your Charlotte Forrest today…and listen carefully to your life for what God has to say because you may be next.

Listen to Your Life

1. As you read this story, who did you think about that made a great impression on you? How did this person make such an impression?

2. What lasting qualities do you have today that you learned from this person?

3. Who is God calling you out to share these lasting qualities with?

Do dogs pray?

A man came to my office one day. I wasn't expecting him so I was a little surprised by his dropping by. Typically, he called first. But when I looked at his face, I knew immediately something was wrong. His dog, his constant companion, was with him.

He stopped by my office to tell me he had prostate cancer and about his plans for surgery. He was obviously numb from the news he had received just minutes before. I asked if I could pray with him. He said, "Yes, please" so I moved to a chair beside him. I took his hand in mine and began to pray.

His dog was seated at his feet. As I held the man's hand in mine and began to pray, I felt the dog put her paw on top of both of our hands where she kept it through the entire prayer. When I said the "Amen," we both looked at this man's best friend who had seemingly held our hands and prayed with us. And the man, with tears in his eyes, said, "She understands."

Now, did that dog pray with us? Or, was she just shaking as she had been taught in obedience school?

I can only tell you this—if God created all of life and declared it good, then animals like this dog just may be a man's best friend. Did she pray like we did? Of course not. Did this man believe she understood that something was worrying him? Yes, of course. Was her action a comfort to him? You better believe it.

Was God involved in this comfort? What's important is this man believed so and experienced God's comfort as he listened to his life that day for what God had to say.

You can do the same today as you listen to life for what God can say to you through the dogs and cats, birds and other animals. You may be surprised at the comfort you receive.

Listen to Your Life

1. What animals do you have that are special to you?

2. How do you enjoy spending time with your animal?

3. Does God comfort you through your animal? How?

What is *Listen to Life?*

Listen to Life is a non-profit, tax-exempt organization whose purpose is to connect people to God by transforming life into a spiritual adventure. We do this through stories about everyday life written by Dr. Joey Faucette, President, in which he has experienced God's love.

The transforming media *Listen to Life* currently uses for sharing these stories are:

1) a syndicated radio show, *Listen to Life with Dr. Joey Faucette*. These 60-second, advertiser-sponsored programs air weekdays on all kinds of radio stations across the nation. Folger Entertainment Company syndicates the show. Joel Folger is the president/CEO and can be reached at 4104 Grace Lane, Grapevine, Texas 76051, (817) 545-3113 or email him at **joel@boldnewradio.com**. Their web site is **www.boldnewradio.com**.

2) a syndicated newspaper column, *Listen to Life with Dr. Joey Faucette*. Across the nation, the newspaper column is the printed text of the same weekday story that airs on the radio show. It also is advertiser-sponsored. Currently, *Listen to Life* is syndicating the column.

3) a web site at **www.listentolife.org**. This site contains more information about *Listen to Life*. Featured on this site is the same day's story that appears in the newspaper column and is heard on the radio show. Not only is the text available, but an audio file, also. Hundreds of persons internationally receive email links to these stories weekdays. If you would like to receive the weekday email links, go to the web site to sign up.

4) speaking engagements. Dr. Faucette speaks to many different groups each year, connecting people with God's love through everyday stories. The groups include businesses, civic groups, and faith communities.

5) books like this one.

To find out more about *Listen to Life* or inquire about any of these transforming media, write us at *Listen to Life*, 3321 Pleasant Gap Drive, Dry Fork, Virginia 24549 or email us at **listentolife@gamewood.net**.

Who is Dr. Joey Faucette?

Well, the short answer is I'm a lot like you. I struggle every day with most of the same life stuff you do — to love my wife and daughters in the ways they need, to pay my mortgage and other bills, to get meaning and purpose from my vocation, and generally to stay connected to God by listening to life.

The long answer—not too long though—is that I've got plenty of formal and informal education degrees. I've done everything from pumping gas at a service station and being a DJ in a nightclub to being a morning air personality and general sales manager of a radio station to freelance writing and pastoring churches for the last eighteen years.

I believe that God has this intense desire to connect with all of us, to be in a personal, intimate relationship with us, and will do whatever it takes to get our attention. God will go out of the Divine Way to talk with us—things like creating unforgettable sunrises and sunsets, inspiring great music, giving us special people in our lives to love, and also, as our daughters remind me, creating dogs like our Charlie, cats like our Maybelle and Norman, and horses like their Sugar and Leo. That's how much God wants to be with us personally!

Unfortunately most of us run right by the sun's rising and setting, turn a deaf ear to the music, take for granted the loving people, and kick the dog who chases the cats who scratch the horse's leg that all live in the house we build daily.

But the take-away here, what I want you to remember about who I am, is this: God's plan for my life is to connect you with God by transforming your life into a spiritual adventure. That's why, out of six billion people on earth, God made me. *Listen to Life with Dr. Joey Faucette* is the expression of that.